Ketamine Therapy Guide for Beginners

Understanding the Basics of Ketamine Therapy

By

Tierney Valen

Copyright@2023

Table of Contents

CHAPTER 1

Introduction

1.1 What is Ketamine?

Ketamine is a powerful anesthetic and dissociative drug that has been used for decades in medical and veterinary settings. It was first synthesized in 1962 by Dr. Calvin Stevens, a scientist working for Parke-Davis, and it quickly gained recognition for its unique pharmacological properties. Ketamine belongs to the class of drugs known as arylcyclohexylamines and acts primarily as an NMDA receptor antagonist. This means it interferes with the normal functioning of a neurotransmitter called glutamate, which is involved in learning, memory, and perception.

Ketamine is renowned for its ability to induce a trance-like state in the user, during which they may experience dissociation from their physical body and surroundings. It is also known for its fast onset of action, making it a valuable tool in emergency medicine and surgery. In medical practice, ketamine has been widely employed as an anesthetic agent for various procedures, particularly in cases where rapid sedation and pain relief are necessary, such as in trauma or during certain surgeries.

In recent years, ketamine has garnered increasing attention for its potential in treating a range of mental health conditions and chronic pain syndromes. When administered at lower doses than those typically used in anesthesia, ketamine can produce a unique and rapid antidepressant effect. This has led to the emergence of "Ketamine Therapy" as a novel and promising approach to the treatment of conditions like depression, anxiety disorders, post-traumatic stress disorder (PTSD), and chronic pain.

Ketamine's potential as a psychiatric treatment has been a subject of extensive research, and it is administered through a variety of routes, including intravenous infusion, intramuscular injection, intranasal spray, and even oral formulations. This diversity in administration methods allows for customization of treatment plans to suit individual patient needs.

1.2 The History of Ketamine Therapy

The history of ketamine therapy is an intriguing journey that spans decades and encompasses various applications. Ketamine's initial development as an anesthetic agent marked the beginning of its medical use. It was first introduced for human use in the 1960s and quickly became a widely accepted and essential tool in surgery and emergency medicine, especially in situations where other anesthetics were less practical due to their slower onset of action.

Over the years, ketamine has been employed not only in traditional medical settings but also in military and field medicine due to its portability and effectiveness. However, it was its unique psychotropic properties, discovered alongside its anesthetic effects, that led to further exploration in the realm of psychiatry and mental health.

In the early 2000s, researchers began to investigate ketamine's potential as a rapid-acting antidepressant. Studies demonstrated that low-dose ketamine infusion could alleviate depressive symptoms in a matter of hours, a stark contrast to traditional antidepressants that often take weeks to produce noticeable effects. This discovery marked a significant turning point in the history of ketamine therapy, as it gave rise to the concept of using ketamine as a novel treatment for mood disorders.

As the body of evidence supporting ketamine therapy's efficacy in treating conditions like depression and PTSD grew, more clinics and healthcare providers started offering ketamine-assisted treatments. The U.S. Food and Drug Administration (FDA) approved a ketamine-derived nasal spray, esketamine, for treatment-resistant depression in 2019, further legitimizing ketamine's role in mental healthcare.

The history of ketamine therapy is still unfolding, with ongoing research, clinical trials, and an expanding body of knowledge. It represents an exciting intersection of neuroscience, psychopharmacology, and mental health treatment, and it continues to evolve as a promising option for individuals who have not responded to conventional therapies.

CHAPTER 2

Understanding Ketamine

2.1 Pharmacology of Ketamine

Ketamine's pharmacology is complex and intriguing, contributing to its diverse range of applications. This section provides an overview of the drug's pharmacological characteristics:

- **Chemical Structure**: Ketamine is a racemic mixture, meaning it consists of equal parts of two enantiomers: R-ketamine and S-ketamine. The S-ketamine enantiomer has been of particular interest due to its potential as a more potent and selective antidepressant.

- **NMDA Receptor Antagonism**: Ketamine primarily functions as a non-competitive antagonist of the NMDA (N-methyl-D-aspartate) receptor, a type of glutamate receptor in the brain. By blocking NMDA receptors, ketamine disrupts the normal functioning of glutamate, leading to its dissociative and anesthetic effects.

- **Glutamate Modulation**: Beyond NMDA receptor antagonism, ketamine also influences other neurotransmitter systems. It enhances the release of glutamate, promoting synaptic plasticity and potentially playing a role in its rapid antidepressant effects.

- **Neurotransmitter Activity**: Ketamine's actions extend to other neurotransmitters, such as serotonin, dopamine, and norepinephrine. These interactions contribute to its mood-altering and psychotomimetic effects.

- **Metabolism**: Ketamine is metabolized in the liver, primarily by the cytochrome P450 enzyme system. It has a relatively short half-life, and its metabolites, including norketamine, may also have pharmacological activity.

- **Route of Administration**: Ketamine can be administered

through various routes,
including intravenous (IV),
intramuscular (IM), intranasal
(IN), and oral. The choice of
administration method affects
the drug's onset of action,
duration, and intensity of
effects.

2.2 Mechanisms of Action

Understanding how ketamine exerts
its effects is critical to its use in both
anesthesia and psychiatric treatment.
This section explores the mechanisms
by which ketamine acts on the brain:

- **NMDA Receptor Blockade**:
  Ketamine's primary mechanism
  of action is the antagonism of
  NMDA receptors. By blocking

these receptors, it interferes with the normal processing of sensory information and perception, resulting in dissociation from one's surroundings and body.

- **Synaptic Plasticity**: Ketamine's ability to enhance glutamate release and promote synaptic plasticity is thought to underlie its rapid antidepressant effects. This increased plasticity is believed to facilitate the formation of new neural connections and the restructuring of dysfunctional ones.

- **BDNF Release**: Ketamine administration has been associated with an increase in brain-derived neurotrophic factor (BDNF) levels. BDNF is a protein that plays a crucial role in neuronal growth, survival, and synaptic plasticity, potentially contributing to ketamine's antidepressant properties.

- **GABAergic Activity**: Ketamine also influences the inhibitory neurotransmitter GABA (gamma-aminobutyric acid). It may increase GABAergic signaling, leading to sedative and anxiolytic effects.

2.3 Different Forms of Ketamine

Ketamine is available in various forms for medical and recreational use, and the choice of form can significantly impact its effects and applications:

- **Intravenous (IV) Ketamine**: IV ketamine is often used in surgical and emergency settings. It provides a rapid onset of anesthesia, making it valuable for procedures where immediate sedation and analgesia are required.

- **Intramuscular (IM) Ketamine**: IM ketamine is another option for rapid sedation and is often used when IV access is unavailable or impractical.

- **Intranasal (IN) Ketamine**: IN ketamine is increasingly used in psychiatric settings. It offers a non-invasive administration method and is particularly suitable for ketamine therapy for mood disorders.

- **Oral Ketamine**: While less common, oral ketamine formulations are used in some medical contexts, such as preoperative medication, and are being explored for their potential in psychiatric treatment.

- **Ketamine Nasal Spray (Esketamine)**: Esketamine, the S-enantiomer of ketamine, is available as a nasal spray and has gained FDA approval for the treatment of treatment-resistant depression. It offers a convenient and standardized way to administer ketamine in a clinical setting.

Understanding the pharmacology, mechanisms of action, and forms of ketamine is crucial for its safe and effective use in various medical and therapeutic applications. Each form and route of administration serves specific purposes and has distinct characteristics, making ketamine a versatile tool in both anesthesia and mental health treatment.

CHAPTER 3

The Science of Ketamine Therapy

3.1 Treatment Indications

Ketamine therapy has demonstrated its potential in treating a variety of medical and mental health conditions. This section provides an overview of its primary treatment indications:

- **Depression**: Ketamine therapy has shown remarkable success in rapidly alleviating symptoms of major depressive disorder (MDD), including treatment-resistant depression. It may also be effective for bipolar

depression, postpartum
depression, and other forms of
depressive disorders.

- **Anxiety Disorders**: Ketamine
  has been explored as a
  treatment for various anxiety
  disorders, such as generalized
  anxiety disorder (GAD), social
  anxiety disorder, and panic
  disorder. It can provide rapid
  relief from anxiety symptoms.

- **Post-Traumatic Stress
  Disorder (PTSD)**: Some
  clinical studies and anecdotal
  evidence suggest that ketamine
  therapy may help individuals
  with PTSD by reducing the
  intensity of traumatic memories
  and improving overall well-
  being.

- **Chronic Pain**: Ketamine has
  long been used as an analgesic
  and may be beneficial for
  individuals with chronic pain
  conditions, including complex
  regional pain syndrome
  (CRPS), fibromyalgia, and
  neuropathic pain.

- **Substance Use Disorders**:
  Emerging research suggests
  that ketamine therapy may
  assist in treating certain
  substance use disorders,
  including alcohol use disorder
  and opioid use disorder. It can
  help reduce cravings and
  withdrawal symptoms.

- **Obsessive-Compulsive
  Disorder (OCD)**: Ketamine
  has been investigated as a
  potential treatment for OCD,
  offering relief from intrusive

thoughts and compulsive behaviors.

- **Mood Disorders**: In addition to depression and anxiety, ketamine therapy may benefit individuals with mood disorders, such as bipolar disorder and rapid-cycling bipolar disorder.

- **Suicidal Ideation**: Ketamine's rapid antidepressant effects have made it a potential intervention for individuals at risk of suicide, providing quick relief from suicidal thoughts.

- **Neuropsychiatric Conditions**: There is ongoing research into the use of ketamine therapy for other neuropsychiatric conditions, such as borderline personality disorder and eating disorders.

3.2 Research and Clinical Studies

Ketamine therapy has attracted significant research interest, leading to a growing body of scientific literature. This section explores the research and clinical studies that have contributed to our understanding of ketamine's therapeutic potential:

- **Antidepressant Effects**: Numerous clinical trials have investigated ketamine's rapid and robust antidepressant effects. Research has explored the optimal dosing, treatment protocols, and long-term outcomes for depression.

- **Mechanisms of Action**: Studies have delved into the neurobiological mechanisms underlying ketamine's antidepressant actions. This includes its impact on glutamate neurotransmission, synaptic plasticity, and brain-derived neurotrophic factor (BDNF) release.

- **Safety and Side Effects**: Research has assessed the safety profile of ketamine therapy, examining potential side effects and adverse reactions. This includes investigations into the risk of dissociation, hallucinations, and abuse potential.

- **Long-Term Efficacy**: Long-term studies have examined the sustainability of ketamine therapy's effects and its potential for relapse prevention in mood disorders.

- **PTSD and Anxiety Disorders**: Clinical trials have explored ketamine's utility in PTSD and various anxiety disorders, shedding light on its potential as a therapeutic intervention.

- **Chronic Pain Management**: Research has investigated ketamine's role in the management of chronic pain conditions, evaluating its analgesic effects and long-term benefits.

3.3 Efficacy and Safety

Ketamine therapy has demonstrated both efficacy and safety in clinical practice. This section provides an overview of these important aspects:

- **Efficacy**: Ketamine therapy is known for its rapid onset of action in treating depression and other mental health conditions. Patients often report significant improvements in mood, reduced suicidal ideation, and increased overall well-being within hours to days after treatment. The effectiveness of ketamine therapy, especially for treatment-resistant cases, has been a game-changer in psychiatric care.

- **Safety**: When administered by trained healthcare professionals in a controlled clinical setting, ketamine therapy is generally considered safe. However, it is not without potential side effects, including dissociation, hallucinations, nausea, and transient blood pressure changes. The risk of adverse events is typically low but should be carefully monitored.

- **Abuse Potential**: Ketamine has a history of recreational use and abuse, which has raised concerns about its potential for misuse. Clinics and providers are vigilant about patient selection and monitoring to mitigate this risk.

- **Long-Term Outcomes**: The long-term effectiveness of ketamine therapy is an ongoing area of research. While it can provide rapid relief, the durability of its effects and the need for maintenance treatments vary from patient to patient.

- **Patient Selection**: The selection of suitable candidates for ketamine therapy is essential. Clinicians typically consider factors such as the severity of the condition, previous treatment history, and medical history in determining if ketamine therapy is appropriate.

The science of ketamine therapy continues to evolve, with ongoing research and clinical experience providing valuable insights into its therapeutic potential and safety considerations. The balance between efficacy and safety is crucial in optimizing its use as a treatment option for various conditions.

CHAPTER 4

The Ketamine Experience

4.1 What to Expect During a Ketamine Session

Ketamine therapy sessions are conducted in a clinical setting with trained healthcare professionals. Understanding what to expect during a ketamine session is crucial for those considering this treatment:

- **Intake and Assessment**: Before the session, you'll typically undergo an intake assessment where your medical and mental health history is reviewed. This helps the healthcare provider determine the appropriate dose and treatment plan.

- **Preparation**: You may be provided with guidelines for preparing for the session, including fasting for a certain period before treatment.

- **Comfortable Environment**: Ketamine sessions are typically conducted in a comfortable and quiet room. You'll recline in a chair or on a bed.

- **Administration**: Ketamine can be administered through various routes, such as intravenous (IV), intramuscular (IM), or intranasal (IN), depending on the clinic and your treatment plan.

- **Monitoring**: Throughout the session, a healthcare professional will monitor your vital signs, including blood pressure, heart rate, and oxygen saturation.

- **Duration**: A typical ketamine session lasts around 45 minutes to an hour, with the effects usually peaking within the first 20-30 minutes.

- **Experience**: During the session, you may experience altered states of consciousness, which can include dissociation from your surroundings and a range of psychological effects. The experience is often described as dream-like or introspective.

- **Post-Session Integration**:
  After the session, you'll have a period of post-session integration, where you can discuss your experience with a therapist or healthcare provider. This is an essential part of the therapeutic process.

4.2 Psychological and Physical Effects

Ketamine's effects can vary from person to person and depend on factors such as the dose, route of administration, and individual response. Here are some common psychological and physical effects associated with ketamine therapy:

- **Psychological Effects**:

- **Dissociation**: Many people experience a sense of dissociation, where they feel detached from their body or surroundings.

- **Altered Perception**: Ketamine can lead to changes in perception, including visual and auditory distortions.

- **Emotional Release**: Some individuals report experiencing intense emotions and memories during the session.

- **Mindfulness**: Ketamine may enhance mindfulness and introspection, allowing for deep self-reflection.

- **Reduced Anxiety**: It can provide relief from anxiety, and some patients describe feeling more at ease.

- **Physical Effects**:

  - **Sedation**: Ketamine often induces a sense of relaxation and drowsiness.

  - **Numbness**: Some people may feel numbness in their extremities.

  - **Changes in Blood Pressure**: Ketamine can cause temporary increases in blood pressure and heart rate, which are closely monitored during the session.

- **Nausea**: Nausea and vomiting are potential side effects but can often be managed with antiemetics.

- **Duration of Effects**: The duration of ketamine's effects can vary, with the psychological effects typically subsiding within a couple of hours. Some individuals may experience lingering effects for the rest of the day, such as improved mood and reduced depressive symptoms.

4.3 Managing Potential Side Effects

Ketamine therapy is generally safe when administered by trained professionals, but there are potential side effects to be aware of. Here's how to manage them:

- **Dissociation**: Dissociation, while a desired effect during therapy, can be disconcerting for some. Your healthcare provider will guide you through the experience, helping you remain calm and grounded.

- **Nausea**: If you experience nausea, inform your provider. They may offer antiemetic medications to alleviate this discomfort.

- **Psychological Distress**: Occasionally, individuals may have challenging psychological experiences during a session. Having a trained therapist or healthcare provider present to provide support and reassurance is essential.

- **Hallucinations**: Hallucinatory experiences can occur, but they are typically mild and transient. If they cause distress, communication with the healthcare provider can help manage them.

- **Blood Pressure and Heart Rate Changes**: Ketamine can temporarily elevate blood pressure and heart rate. Monitoring and adjustment of the dose can help mitigate this effect.

- **Post-Session Care**: After the session, you may feel groggy or disoriented. It's advisable to have someone accompany you and ensure you have a safe and supportive environment for the rest of the day.

Managing potential side effects during a ketamine therapy session involves close communication with your healthcare provider and adherence to their guidance. The therapy is designed to provide a supportive and therapeutic environment to maximize its benefits while minimizing any discomfort or adverse effects.

CHAPTER 5

Conditions Treated with Ketamine Therapy

5.1 Depression

Ketamine therapy has gained significant attention for its efficacy in treating various forms of depression, including:

- **Major Depressive Disorder (MDD)**: Ketamine has shown rapid and robust antidepressant effects, making it a promising option for individuals with MDD, particularly those who have not responded to conventional antidepressants.

- **Bipolar Depression**: Ketamine therapy may be used as an adjunctive treatment for bipolar depression, helping to alleviate depressive symptoms in individuals with bipolar disorder.

- **Postpartum Depression**: Ketamine has been explored as a potential intervention for postpartum depression, providing relief for new mothers struggling with severe mood disturbances.

- **Seasonal Affective Disorder (SAD)**: Individuals with SAD, a type of depression related to changes in seasons, may find relief from their symptoms through ketamine therapy.

- **Treatment-Resistant Depression**: Ketamine is especially valuable for individuals with treatment-resistant depression, where traditional antidepressants have not been effective. It offers a rapid and often sustained response in such cases.

5.2 Anxiety Disorders

Anxiety disorders can be debilitating, and ketamine therapy has shown promise in treating several anxiety-related conditions, including:

- **Generalized Anxiety Disorder (GAD)**: Ketamine therapy may help reduce the symptoms of excessive worry, fear, and anxiety that are characteristic of GAD.

- **Social Anxiety Disorder**: Individuals with social anxiety disorder may experience relief from their fear of social interactions and performance-related anxiety through ketamine treatment.

- **Panic Disorder**: Ketamine can help alleviate panic attacks and the accompanying sense of impending doom or terror that characterizes panic disorder.

- **Specific Phobias**: People with specific phobias may find relief from their intense and irrational fears through ketamine therapy.

5.3 Post-Traumatic Stress Disorder (PTSD)

Post-Traumatic Stress Disorder is a complex condition resulting from exposure to traumatic events. Ketamine therapy has been investigated as a potential treatment for PTSD:

- **Trauma-Related Symptoms**: Ketamine may help individuals with PTSD by reducing the intensity of traumatic memories and the emotional distress associated with them.

- **Emotional Processing**: Ketamine's ability to facilitate emotional processing may help individuals with PTSD confront and process their traumatic experiences more effectively.

- **Anxiety and Hyperarousal**: Ketamine can assist in reducing symptoms of anxiety, hypervigilance, and exaggerated startle responses often seen in PTSD.

It's important to note that while ketamine therapy shows promise for these conditions, it is not a first-line treatment. It is typically considered when other treatments have proven ineffective, and it is administered under the supervision of qualified healthcare professionals in a clinical setting. The choice to pursue ketamine therapy should be made in consultation with a healthcare provider, taking into account individual circumstances and treatment history.

5.4 Chronic Pain

Ketamine has a long history of use as an analgesic and can be a valuable option for managing chronic pain conditions, including:

- **Complex Regional Pain Syndrome (CRPS)**: Ketamine therapy has shown effectiveness in reducing the symptoms of CRPS, a chronic pain condition that often affects the limbs and can be associated with significant discomfort and disability.

- **Fibromyalgia**: Individuals with fibromyalgia, a condition characterized by widespread pain, may find relief from their symptoms through ketamine therapy.

- **Neuropathic Pain**: Ketamine can be used in the management of neuropathic pain, which often results from nerve damage and can be challenging to treat with traditional analgesics.

- **Migraines**: Ketamine infusions have been explored as a treatment option for severe and treatment-resistant migraines.

5.5 Substance Use Disorders

Ketamine therapy is being investigated as a potential treatment for certain substance use disorders, offering a unique approach to addiction management:

- **Alcohol Use Disorder (AUD)**: Research has shown that ketamine may help reduce alcohol cravings and withdrawal symptoms, making it a possible adjunct to traditional AUD treatment strategies.

- **Opioid Use Disorder (OUD)**: Ketamine has been studied for its role in managing OUD, particularly in reducing opioid cravings and withdrawal discomfort.

- **Other Addictions**: While the focus has primarily been on alcohol and opioid use disorders, ketamine therapy's potential for other substance use disorders is also being explored.

5.6 Other Applications

Ketamine therapy has a range of other potential applications, though these may be subject to ongoing research and clinical trials:

- **Eating Disorders**: Ketamine is being investigated for its potential in treating eating disorders, such as anorexia nervosa and bulimia nervosa, by addressing underlying mood and anxiety symptoms.

- **Borderline Personality Disorder (BPD)**: Some research suggests that ketamine may have a role in managing mood instability and impulsivity in individuals with BPD.

- **Chronic Suicidal Ideation**: Ketamine's rapid-acting

antidepressant effects have made it a focal point in the management of individuals experiencing chronic suicidal ideation, offering immediate relief.

- **Neuropsychiatric Conditions**: Ketamine's unique pharmacological properties may be applicable to other neuropsychiatric conditions, and research continues to explore its potential in these areas.

It's important to emphasize that while ketamine therapy holds promise for these conditions and applications, it is still a relatively novel approach, and research is ongoing. Decisions about using ketamine therapy for these conditions should be made in consultation with healthcare professionals who are experienced in its administration and tailored to individual patient needs and circumstances.

CHAPTER 6

Ketamine Providers and Clinics

6.1 Finding a Qualified Ketamine Clinic

When looking for a ketamine clinic, it's crucial to ensure that you receive safe and effective treatment. Here are steps to help you find a qualified clinic:

- **Consult with Your Primary Care Physician**: Start by discussing your interest in ketamine therapy with your primary care physician or mental health provider. They may be able to provide recommendations or referrals to reputable clinics.

- **Research Online**: Conduct online research to identify ketamine clinics in your area. Look for clinics that have established a professional online presence and positive reviews or testimonials.

- **Check Credentials and Licenses**: Ensure that the clinic and its healthcare providers have the necessary licenses and certifications to administer ketamine therapy. This may include licenses for medical doctors, registered nurses, or nurse practitioners.

- **Ask for Referrals**: Seek recommendations from trusted sources, such as friends, family,

or support groups, who may
have experience with ketamine
therapy or know of reputable
clinics.

- **Verify Experience**: Inquire
  about the clinic's experience in
  administering ketamine
  therapy. Clinics with a history
  of providing such treatments
  may be more adept at ensuring
  safety and effectiveness.

- **Ask About Treatment
  Protocols**: Find out about the
  clinic's treatment protocols,
  including dosing,
  administration methods, and
  monitoring during sessions.
  Clinics that follow evidence-
  based guidelines may offer
  more reliable treatments.

- **Consultation and Assessment**: Ensure that the clinic conducts thorough assessments and consultations before initiating treatment to determine whether ketamine therapy is a suitable option for your condition.

- **Transparency and Informed Consent**: The clinic should be transparent about the treatment process, potential risks, benefits, and costs. Informed consent should be obtained before treatment.

- **Safety Protocols**: Ask about the clinic's safety protocols, including monitoring during sessions, emergency procedures, and the presence of healthcare professionals.

- **Collaboration with Mental Health Professionals**: Many clinics work in collaboration with mental health professionals or therapists to provide a comprehensive treatment approach. Inquire about these partnerships.

CHAPTER 7

Preparing for Ketamine Therapy

7.1 Initial Consultation

The initial consultation is a crucial step in preparing for ketamine therapy. It allows you and the healthcare provider to discuss your treatment goals, medical history, and expectations. Here's what to expect during this phase:

- **Discussion of Treatment Goals**: During the initial consultation, you'll discuss the specific mental health condition or symptoms you're seeking to address with ketamine therapy. Be open and honest about your

treatment goals and
expectations.

- **Medical History Review**: The
  healthcare provider will
  conduct a thorough review of
  your medical history. This
  includes information about past
  and current medical conditions,
  medications, allergies, and any
  surgical history.

- **Psychiatric Evaluation**: You'll
  undergo a psychiatric
  evaluation to assess your
  mental health condition and any
  comorbidities, such as
  depression or anxiety disorders.

- **Discussion of Medications**:
  Inform the provider about any
  medications you're currently
  taking. Some medications may

interact with ketamine, and adjustments may be necessary.

- **Informed Consent**: The provider will explain the treatment process, potential risks, and benefits. Informed consent is typically obtained during this phase, ensuring that you fully understand what the treatment entails.

- **Addressing Questions and Concerns**: Use this opportunity to ask questions and address any concerns you may have about ketamine therapy.

- **Assessment of Suitability**: The healthcare provider will assess whether ketamine therapy is a suitable treatment option for your specific condition and individual circumstances.

7.2 Medical and Psychological Assessments

Before starting ketamine therapy, a series of medical and psychological assessments are typically conducted to ensure your safety and the appropriateness of the treatment:

- **Physical Examination**: You may undergo a physical examination to assess your overall health, including vital signs, heart rate, blood pressure, and general well-being.

- **Laboratory Tests**: Blood tests and other laboratory assessments may be performed to check for any underlying medical conditions, evaluate organ function, and ensure that you are in good health for the therapy.

- **Psychological Assessment**: A psychological evaluation helps the healthcare provider understand your mental health condition, symptom severity, and any underlying psychological factors that may contribute to your condition.

- **Mental Health Assessment**: In addition to a general psychological assessment, specific mental health assessments may be conducted to diagnose and assess the severity of conditions like depression or anxiety.

- **Assessment of Current Medications**: The provider will review any current medications

to identify potential interactions
or contraindications with
ketamine therapy.

- **Monitoring of Comorbidities**:
  If you have any co-occurring
  conditions or comorbidities,
  such as substance use disorders
  or eating disorders, these will
  be assessed to determine the
  best course of treatment.

- **Safety Assessment**: The
  healthcare provider will assess
  whether you have any risk
  factors or contraindications that
  may affect the safety of
  ketamine therapy.

7.3 Pre-session Guidelines

Preparation for your ketamine therapy sessions is essential to ensure a safe and effective experience. Here are some pre-session guidelines to follow:

- **Fasting**: Depending on the clinic's protocol, you may be asked to fast for a certain period before your ketamine session. This helps minimize the risk of nausea, which can be a side effect of ketamine.

- **Hydration**: Staying well-hydrated is important. Make sure to drink enough water in the hours leading up to the session.

- **Medication Review**: If you are taking any medications, discuss with your healthcare provider whether any adjustments are necessary before the session.

- **Comfortable Clothing**: Wear comfortable clothing to the session, as you'll be reclining or lying down during the treatment.

- **Arrival Time**: Arrive on time for your session to allow for any necessary preparations or assessments before treatment.

- **Mental Preparation**: Mentally prepare yourself for the experience. Setting intentions and mentally focusing on your treatment goals can be helpful.

- **Transportation**: Arrange for transportation to and from the clinic, as you may not be in a condition to drive after the session.

- **Supportive Companion**: Having a supportive friend or family member accompany you to the session and drive you home afterward can provide reassurance and assistance.

- **Post-Session Rest**: After the session, plan to rest and recover. Avoid strenuous activities for the rest of the day.

Following these pre-session guidelines and completing the necessary assessments and consultations will help ensure a safe and productive experience with ketamine therapy. It's important to follow the guidance of your healthcare provider throughout the entire process.

CHAPTER 8

The Ketamine Therapy Process

8.1 The Treatment Session

The ketamine treatment session is the core of the therapy, where you receive the medication and experience its effects. Here's what to expect during a typical session:

- **Preparation**: Before the session, you'll arrive at the clinic and may have some time to prepare. This could involve reviewing your treatment goals and any questions or concerns you have with the healthcare provider.

- **Administration**: Ketamine can be administered through various routes, including intravenous (IV), intramuscular (IM), or intranasal (IN), depending on the clinic's protocol and your specific treatment plan.

- **Session Duration**: A ketamine session usually lasts around 45 minutes to an hour, with the effects typically peaking within the first 20-30 minutes. During this time, you'll be in a comfortable and quiet environment, such as a reclining chair or bed.

- **Monitoring**: Throughout the session, a healthcare provider or nurse will monitor your vital signs, including blood pressure, heart rate, and oxygen saturation, to ensure your safety.

- **Experience**: You'll experience the psychological and physical effects of ketamine, which may include dissociation, altered perception, emotional release, and relaxation. It's essential to remain as relaxed and open as possible during this phase.

- **Post-Session Rest**: After the session, you may be asked to rest for a short period. It's common to feel groggy, disoriented, or introspective after the treatment.

8.2 Integration and Follow-up

Integration and follow-up are critical components of ketamine therapy to help you process the experience and track your progress:

- **Integration Session**: After the ketamine session, you'll typically have an integration session with a therapist or healthcare provider. This is a time to discuss and process your experiences, emotions, and insights during the session.

- **Tracking Progress**: Over the course of your treatment, you'll work with your healthcare provider to monitor your progress. Regular sessions may be scheduled to assess how the treatment is affecting your symptoms and overall well-being.

- **Adjustments**: Based on your progress, the treatment plan may be adjusted. This could involve modifying the dosage, frequency of sessions, or other aspects of the treatment.

- **Mental Health Support**: Throughout the treatment process, you'll continue to receive mental health support, which may include psychotherapy or counseling, to address the underlying issues contributing to your condition.

8.3 Treatment Plans and Duration

The treatment plan for ketamine therapy varies depending on individual needs and the specific condition being treated. Here are some general considerations:

- **Frequency of Sessions**: The frequency of ketamine sessions can vary, but initial treatment phases may involve sessions spaced closely together (e.g., multiple sessions over a few weeks) to establish the therapeutic effects. Afterward, maintenance sessions are scheduled at less frequent intervals.

- **Duration**: The duration of ketamine therapy can also vary widely. Some individuals may experience significant improvement after a few sessions, while others may require ongoing maintenance sessions over a more extended period.

- **Maintenance and Relapse Prevention**: Maintenance sessions are often used to prevent relapse and maintain the therapeutic effects of ketamine therapy. The duration and frequency of these sessions are determined on an individual basis.

- **Individualized Approach**: Ketamine therapy is highly individualized. Your healthcare provider will work with you to create a treatment plan tailored to your specific needs and condition.

- **Long-Term Goals**: The goals of ketamine therapy may include not only symptom relief but also improved overall well-being and the development of coping strategies to manage your condition effectively.

- **Combination with Other Treatments**: Ketamine therapy may be used in combination with other treatments, such as psychotherapy, medication, or lifestyle modifications, to optimize the results.

It's important to approach ketamine therapy as part of a comprehensive treatment plan for mental health conditions. Regular communication with your healthcare provider and adherence to the treatment plan are essential for achieving the best outcomes. Ketamine therapy can

provide rapid relief, but long-term
success often involves a holistic
approach to mental health and
wellness.

CHAPTER 9

Potential Risks and Contraindications

9.1 Adverse Effects

Ketamine therapy is generally safe when administered by qualified healthcare professionals in a controlled clinical setting. However, there are potential adverse effects to be aware of:

- **Dissociation**: Dissociation is a common and often desired effect during ketamine therapy. While it can provide insight and therapeutic benefits, it may be disconcerting for some individuals.

- **Hallucinations**: Mild hallucinations or altered perceptions can occur during a session. These experiences are typically transient but may cause distress in some cases.

- **Nausea and Vomiting**: Nausea is a potential side effect of ketamine, but it can often be managed with antiemetic medications. Vomiting can also occur in some cases.

- **Increased Heart Rate and Blood Pressure**: Ketamine can lead to temporary increases in heart rate and blood pressure. Healthcare providers monitor these vital signs during sessions.

- **Headache**: Some individuals may experience mild to

moderate headaches after a ketamine session.

- **Transient Hypertension**: Ketamine can cause transient hypertension (high blood pressure), which is monitored during the session. Individuals with uncontrolled high blood pressure may be at greater risk.

- **Transitory Psychological Distress**: Rarely, individuals may experience psychological distress, including anxiety, paranoia, or agitation during or after a ketamine session.

- **Potential for Misuse**: Ketamine has a history of recreational use and abuse. Clinics and healthcare providers are vigilant about

patient selection and
monitoring to mitigate this risk.

It's essential to note that these adverse effects are typically mild, transient, and manageable in a clinical setting. A healthcare provider's expertise in monitoring and managing these effects is crucial to patient safety.

9.2 Who Should Avoid Ketamine Therapy

Ketamine therapy may not be appropriate for everyone. Some individuals and conditions are considered contraindications for this treatment:

- **Active Psychosis**: Individuals with active psychotic disorders, such as schizophrenia, should generally avoid ketamine therapy, as it may exacerbate psychotic symptoms.

- **Uncontrolled Hypertension**: People with severe or uncontrolled high blood pressure may be at increased risk of hypertensive crises during a ketamine session. It is important to have blood pressure well managed before considering treatment.

- **Active Substance Abuse**: Individuals with a current or recent history of substance abuse may be at higher risk of misuse of ketamine. Careful screening and assessment are necessary to determine suitability.

- **Certain Medical Conditions**: People with certain medical conditions, such as severe cardiovascular disease or a history of stroke, may not be suitable candidates for ketamine therapy.

- **Pregnancy and Breastfeeding**: The safety of ketamine therapy during pregnancy and breastfeeding has not been established, and its use is generally avoided during these periods.

- **Medication Interactions**: Some medications can interact with ketamine, potentially increasing the risk of adverse effects. It's important to discuss current medications with your healthcare provider.

- **Allergy or Sensitivity**: Individuals who have known

allergies or sensitivities to ketamine or its components should not receive ketamine therapy.

- **Unrealistic Expectations**: Ketamine therapy is not a guaranteed cure for mental health conditions. Individuals with unrealistic expectations or a lack of commitment to the process may not be suitable candidates.

It is essential to have a comprehensive assessment and consultation with a qualified healthcare provider to determine if ketamine therapy is appropriate for your specific situation. The provider will consider your medical and psychiatric history, current symptoms, and individual risk factors when making this determination.

CHAPTER 10

Research and Future Developments

10.1 Ongoing Ketamine Studies

Ketamine therapy continues to be the subject of ongoing research, as scientists and clinicians explore its potential applications, mechanisms of action, and safety. Some areas of ongoing study include:

- **Mechanisms of Action**: Researchers are delving deeper into the neurobiological mechanisms underlying ketamine's rapid antidepressant effects. Understanding how ketamine works at the molecular and synaptic levels is a key focus.

- **Long-Term Efficacy and Safety**: Studies are assessing the long-term effectiveness and safety of ketamine therapy. This includes investigations into the durability of treatment effects and the potential for relapse.

- **Optimal Dosing and Administration**: Researchers are working to refine dosing protocols, administration methods, and treatment regimens to maximize the benefits of ketamine therapy while minimizing side effects.

- **Combination Therapies**: There is interest in combining

ketamine therapy with other treatment modalities, such as psychotherapy or other medications, to enhance outcomes for various mental health conditions.

- **Ketamine and Suicidality**: Ongoing research is exploring the use of ketamine in the management of chronic suicidal ideation and its role in preventing suicide.

- **Other Psychiatric and Neuropsychiatric Conditions**: Researchers are investigating the potential applications of ketamine therapy in treating a broader range of psychiatric and neuropsychiatric conditions, such as eating disorders and borderline personality disorder.

- **Neuroimaging Studies**: Advanced neuroimaging techniques are being used to gain insights into how ketamine impacts the brain, aiding in the understanding of its effects on mood and cognition.

- **Patient Selection and Predictive Markers**: Efforts are ongoing to identify predictive markers and characteristics that can help determine which individuals are most likely to benefit from ketamine therapy.

10.2 The Future of Ketamine Therapy

The future of ketamine therapy holds promise and potential developments in several areas:

- **Personalized Treatment**: As research advances, treatment plans may become increasingly personalized. Individualized dosing and treatment regimens could optimize results while minimizing side effects.

- **Innovative Delivery Methods**: Researchers are exploring alternative administration methods for ketamine, such as intranasal sprays and lozenges, which may enhance convenience and accessibility.

- **Synthetic Analogs**: Scientists are working on developing synthetic analogs of ketamine with similar antidepressant effects but potentially fewer dissociative and hallucinogenic properties.

- **Insurance Coverage**: As more clinical evidence accumulates, there may be expanded insurance coverage for ketamine therapy, making it more accessible to a broader range of patients.

- **Regulatory Approvals**: Continued research may lead to expanded regulatory approvals for ketamine and its derivatives for specific mental health conditions.

- **Integration with Traditional Psychiatry**: Ketamine therapy may become more integrated into traditional psychiatric treatment plans, serving as an adjunct to existing therapies.

- **Telemedicine and Accessibility**: The development of telemedicine practices may enhance the accessibility of ketamine therapy, making it available to individuals in remote or underserved areas.

- **Reduction in Stigma**: As ketamine therapy becomes more widely accepted, the stigma associated with it and other psychedelic-assisted therapies may diminish, encouraging more individuals to seek help for mental health conditions.

It's important to note that the field of ketamine therapy is rapidly evolving, and ongoing research will continue to shape its future. Patients considering ketamine therapy should consult with qualified healthcare providers to stay informed about the latest developments and determine the most suitable treatment options for their specific needs.

www.ingramcontent.com/pod-product-compliance
Lightning Source LLC
Chambersburg PA
CBHW050833260726
48660CB00006B/2221